P9-DGD-258

ESSENTIAL TIPS

101

BARBECUING

ESSENTIAL TIPS
101

BARBECUING

Marlena Spieler

DK PUBLISHING, INC.

A DK PUBLISHING BOOK

Editor Bella Pringle
Art Editor Colin Walton
Senior Editor Gillian Roberts
Series Art Editor Alison Donovan
Production Controller Jenny May
US Editor Ray Rogers

Follow either imperial or metric units throughout a recipe,
never a mixture of the two, since they are not exact equivalents.

First American Edition, 1998
4 6 8 10 9 7 5 3
Published in the United States by DK Publishing, Inc.
95 Madison Avenue, New York, New York 10016

Visit us on the World Wide Web at http://www.dk.com

Copyright © 1998 Dorling Kindersley Limited, London

All rights reserved under International and Pan-American Copyright Conventions.
No part of this publication may be reproduced, stored in a retrieval system,
or transmitted in any form or by any means, electronic, mechanical, photocopying,
recording, or otherwise, without the prior written permission of the copyright owner.
Published in Great Britain by Dorling Kindersley Limited.

ISBN 0-7894-2780-X

Text film output by R&B Creative Services Ltd, Great Britain
Reproduced by Colourscan, Singapore
Printed and bound in Italy by Graphicom

ESSENTIAL TIPS

BARBECUING KNOW-HOW

1 WHAT IS BARBECUING?

Barbecuing is a simple method of cooking outdoors. Meat, fish, and vegetables are cooked on a grate or grill over an open fire and quickly absorb the aroma of the smoke, which gives the food its distinct flavor.

◁ BEEF KEBABS (TIP 81)

2 WHERE TO PLACE YOUR BARBECUE

For safety, always place a stand-up barbecue on a firm, level surface so that, once lit, it will not be able to topple over. Place portable models on the ground or on a heatproof surface, but not on a table. Keep all barbecues safely away from garden fences, trees, hedges, dry leaves, or any object that could catch a falling spark from the fire and ignite.

3 DIFFERENT KINDS OF BARBECUE

A sophisticated range of barbecues is available. The following review should help you decide which one suits your needs, depending on the number of people you cater for and the kind of food you enjoy cooking.

OPEN-TOP MODELS
If you tend to cook meat that needs quick searing over a high heat, these models are ideal; the coals burn hotter due to their exposure to air.

An open-top model to leave outdoors must be rust resistant

Packed up
ready to travel

◁ **PORTABLE**
This is just
right for small
outdoor areas,
for example a
balcony, and it
can be neatly
stowed away.

KETTLE BARBECUE ▷
Ideal for cooking whole legs
of meat and chicken: the
domed lid limits the supply
of air to the fire so that the
food cooks slowly and with
control. The lid also keeps
the smoke inside, increasing
the flavor of the food.

Fold-out legs hold
hot pan base above
ground level

Rounded pan and lid
reflect heat, providing
an even cooking
temperature

DISPOSABLE TRAY ▷
For the occasional
cookout, this
disposable tray is
inexpensive and
portable. The foil pan
comes prepacked with fuel.

△ **GAS BARBECUE**
No mess or fuss with this
model, fueled by butane
gas. The barbecue taste
comes from lava rock,
not charcoal or wood.

4 BARBECUE LIGHTING MATERIALS

Achieving a good fire is the key to a successful barbecue. However, it is often in these early stages that many barbecue users have the most problems. Featured here is a range of lighting materials designed to light coals quickly without giving off fumes that may taint the food. There's also a survey of charcoal and wood fuels available, and help in assessing which may suit your cooking needs; the burning time and heat produced can vary, and some have scented smoke.

LIGHTING MATERIALS
You can light the fire in a number of ways. Firelighters and lighter fluid designed for barbecue use work well. But if you want to have coals hot enough for cooking right away, without using chemicals, place an electric heating element under the coals until they ignite (Tip 9), or pack the coals into a fire chimney and light with newspaper (Tip 10).

△ BARBECUE FIRELIGHTERS

△ LONG SAFETY MATCHES

△ NEWSPAPER

◁ ELECTRIC STARTER (TIP 9)

△ FIRE CHIMNEY (TIP 10)

△ LIGHTER FLUID (TIP 8)

CAUTION!
Use lighter fluid only before the fire has been lit, and then put it away. Always light the fire with long matches so that you can stand well back. Never squirt gas or other fluid that is flammable directly onto the fire since it can flare up, engulfing you in flames.

BARBECUE FUELS

Charcoal and wood are the most commonly sold barbecue fuels. To help you to make an informed choice, their properties are outlined below.

▷ **Lump charcoal** is made from whole pieces of wood, with no filler. It burns hotter and cleaner than briquettes.

◁ **Briquettes** contain sawdust, coal, and sand, bound together with a petroleum-based substance. Once lit, they can burn longer than lump charcoal.

▷ **Mesquite charcoal** has a woody scent and burns cleanly.

◁ **Wood fires** are difficult to start but then burn quicker than charcoal or briquettes. Fruit wood such as apple has scented smoke.

5 PREPARING THE FIRE

Food is barbecued directly (placed straight on the grill over the heat of the coals) or indirectly (placed on the grill with a drip pan in the fuel bed beneath). The cooking method determines how you prepare the fire.

△ **DIRECT COOKING**
Arrange the coals in a heap, two layers deep if you intend to cook for more than 45–60 minutes, or in just a single layer if you plan to cook a few items quickly.

△ **INDIRECT COOKING**
Place a foil drip pan in the center of the fuel bed. Arrange a heap of coals around the edges of the pan, making sure that they are stacked no higher than its sides.

6 USING KINDLING

The best technique for lighting the barbecue with just kindling is to tear off sheets of newspaper, roll them into tight tubes, and then twist them at both ends. Place the newspaper twists in the bottom of the fuel grate, and lay dry twigs or sticks on top. Over this, arrange the coals in a mound, leaving air spaces between them. Light the newspaper and add more charcoal, piece by piece, as the fire grows.

For safety, use a long match to light paper, and stand well back

7 USING FIRELIGHTERS

Choose firelighter cubes designed for barbecue use. Then, wearing rubber gloves, arrange the charcoal pieces into a pyramid on the grate. Break one or two firelighters in half and place the pieces between the coals. Light the firelighters using a long safety match, so that you can stand well back. They will burn fiercely for a few minutes, allowing time for the charcoal to ignite.

Arrange lumps of charcoal in a pyramid

Take care: firelighters may flare up

8 USING LIGHTER FLUID

Wearing protective gloves, heap the coals into a pyramid and pour a liberal sprinkling of lighter fluid over them. Allow the fluid to soak in for a couple of minutes. Put the fluid away in a safe place before lighting the coals, using a taper so that you can stand at arm's length. Once lit, allow the fluid to burn off before cooking, or it may taint the food with a chemical taste.

Allow coals to absorb fluid

Do not use once the fire is lit

9 USING AN ELECTRIC STARTER

Arrange the fuel in a small heap at the center of the grate. Plug in the electric starter to the nearest outlet (you may need to use an extension cord). Scoop up all the coals in the grate onto the hand-shaped heating element. Within 1–2 minutes, the electric starter will glow red hot, and the coals will ignite. Unplug the starter and remove it to a safe place so it has time to cool down.

Once lit, spread coals over grate

Take care when lifting out hot element

10 USING A FIRE CHIMNEY

Coals are packed into the tall metal cylinder, which is separated by a perforated base from the lighting area below (*Tip 4*). The intense heat of the fire is funneled into the chimney and sets the coals ablaze.

Glowing red-hot coals are ready to use

1 △ Pack the base of the cylinder with newspaper, and then place it on the grate for safety. Fill the top section with coals. Light the newspaper.

2 △ Within 5–10 minutes, some of the coals will be glowing red. When all are glowing, put on a fireproof glove. Carefully pick up the fire chimney by its wooden handle with your gloved hand and tip the hot coals into the grate. Use tongs to spread them out, then you are ready to cook.

11 WHEN CAN YOU START COOKING?

Many kinds of fuel can take about 45 minutes to burn down to the even heat required for cooking, but some coals such as lumpwood charcoal, which has few impurities, are ready for cooking in about 15 minutes. As a general rule, follow the guidelines on the packaging, and if flames are still licking the coals, the fire is not yet ready for use. Also, different kinds of food need to be cooked over different coal heats. For example, lean meats are best seared over red-hot coals, while larger cuts are best cooked over a slower fire to avoid charring.

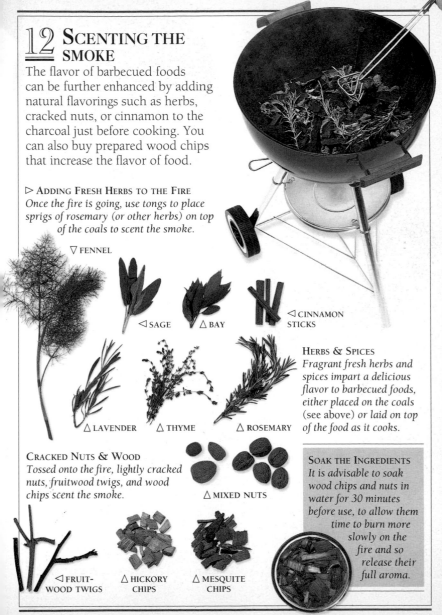

12 SCENTING THE SMOKE

The flavor of barbecued foods can be further enhanced by adding natural flavorings such as herbs, cracked nuts, or cinnamon to the charcoal just before cooking. You can also buy prepared wood chips that increase the flavor of food.

▷ ADDING FRESH HERBS TO THE FIRE
Once the fire is going, use tongs to place sprigs of rosemary (or other herbs) on top of the coals to scent the smoke.

▽ FENNEL

◁ SAGE △ BAY ◁ CINNAMON STICKS

△ LAVENDER △ THYME △ ROSEMARY

HERBS & SPICES
Fragrant fresh herbs and spices impart a delicious flavor to barbecued foods, either placed on the coals (see above) or laid on top of the food as it cooks.

CRACKED NUTS & WOOD
Tossed onto the fire, lightly cracked nuts, fruitwood twigs, and wood chips scent the smoke.

△ MIXED NUTS

◁ FRUIT-WOOD TWIGS △ HICKORY CHIPS △ MESQUITE CHIPS

SOAK THE INGREDIENTS
It is advisable to soak wood chips and nuts in water for 30 minutes before use, to allow them time to burn more slowly on the fire and so release their full aroma.

15

13 USING RED-HOT COALS

At this temperature, food cooks quickly and can burn on the outside while staying raw inside. Sear meat cuts over hot coals to seal in the flavor, or cook lean cuts, such as fish filets, which will cook right through.

Coals have light dusting of white ash

Coals are glowing red: flames have subsided

◁ **GLOWING RED**
The coals are now heated thoroughly and are at their top temperature.

Lamb steaks
are best seared over hot coals (Tip 79).

14 USING MEDIUM-HOT COALS

This temperature suits most foods since pieces of meat, fish, poultry, and vegetables cook best over moderate heat. If food starts to burn, move it to the outer edges of the grill, which are usually cooler.

Thicker layer of white ash now covers coals

Intense red heat has begun to subside

◁ **LAYER OF ASH**
The coals start to burn down and reach a moderate temperature.

Fish steaks
are cooked over a moderate heat (Tip 63).

15 USING COOL COALS

Once the coals have died down, vegetables and fruit can be warmed on the grill with just a light charring of their skin, or cooked in among the coals. Whole chicken and large cuts of meat also taste good when cooked over a cool fire for 1–2 hours but, for best results, a whole chicken should be cooked on a covered barbecue (*Tip 17*).

Coals no longer show any red

Thick layer of ash covers coals

◁ **DYING DOWN**
The coals have burned down but are still very warm.

Potatoes *can be left to cook in a mound of slow coals for 1–2 hours (Tip 46).*

Sour cream with chives makes a mouth-watering accompaniment to the potatoes.

▷ **TESTING THE HEAT**
When the barbecue starts to slow down, you should be able to hold your hand over the grill for about 8 seconds. If you need to pull it away before then, it is still much too hot for slow cooking.

Shallots and cherry tomatoes *can be warmed through as the barbecue cools (Tips 47 & 48).*

17

16 OPEN-TOP BARBECUING

Keep people away from open fire

Barbecuing food on an open grill requires constant vigilance: the fire burns hot since air gets to it. It is easy to burn foods on the outside (especially meats), since hot fat dripping onto the coals causes flare-ups. Foods such as hamburgers cook well in these conditions, since the heat chars the food on the outside, sealing in its juices. For foods that need to be cooked right through, the secret is to move the food to the cooler edges of the grill, or to wait for the heat to die down.

Shrimp cook in minutes over medium-hot to hot coals (Tip 59)

Burgers taste superb chargrilled on an open fire (Tip 76).

Lean pork medallions need searing at high temperatures on an open grill (Tip 83).

17 COVERED BARBECUING

Barbecuing food with the cover pulled down will give you more control if you want to cook food slowly and evenly. This works particularly well for large cuts of meat and whole fish since the cover reflects heat onto all surfaces of the barbecue, and the food cooks on both sides without having to be turned over. Also, food cooking on a covered barbecue will not need to be moved away from hot spots on the grill: you can control the intensity of the heat by opening or closing the air vents in the cover and base of the pan.

Lid and pan contain vents to control draft

Heat from coal is reflected off cover

Chicken pieces cook more evenly under a cover (Tip 67).

▽ **ADJUSTING THE VENTS**
Always wear a heatproof glove before opening or closing the cover vent: the metal is usually very hot and may burn your fingers.

Ribs are more tender the slower they cook (Tip 75).

19

18 USING A DRIP PAN

When cooking a large cut of meat or a whole chicken or other poultry on a covered barbecue, it is a good idea to place a drip pan on the grate below the grill pan to collect the juices for making gravy (*Tip 5*). Before you begin, half-fill the drip pan with water, stock, or wine to help prevent the meat from drying out while it is cooking. At 30-minute intervals, lift the cover of the barbecue and check that the liquid in the drip tray has not evaporated; refill if necessary. Skim the fat off any gravy in the pan before serving it with the meat.

19 SEARING MEAT

A clever way to prevent quick-cooking meat from drying out is to cook it rapidly on both sides to seal in the juices. Finish cooking the meat at the cooler outer edges of the grill.

1 ▷ Using a long-handled basting brush, simply oil the grill rack with vegetable oil so that the meat can be turned without sticking to the metal.

2 △ Using long-handled tongs, place the meat on the center of the grill – the hottest part – and cook for 1–2 minutes on each side to sear it.

3 △ Remove the seared meat to the cooler edge of the grill and continue cooking for 4–5 minutes a side for rare and up to 10 minutes for well done.

20 BARBECUE TOOLS

Buy long-handled tools, preferably with wood rather than metal handles, for putting food on and taking it off the hot grill. An apron protects your clothes, and fireproof gloves allow you to pick up food cooking on metal skewers and adjust the barbecue air vents. A hinged basket for cooking fragile filets of fish is also wise: it will save you the frustration of food slipping through the grill into the fire.

△ SCISSOR-ACTION TONGS

△ LONG-HANDLED TONGS

△ LONG-HANDLED SPATULA

△ LONG-HANDLED FORK

◁ FIREPROOF GLOVES

△ HINGED WIRE BASKET

◁ LARGE APRON

△ FLAT METAL SKEWERS

△ WOODEN SKEWERS

△ HINGED WIRE FISH BASKET

21

21 HOW TO STOKE THE FIRE

If the barbecue appears to be dying down and you want to revive it, simply remove the grill and, using long-handled tongs, pick up the coals in turn and tap off the ash until they start to glow again. If the barbecue has air vents, open them wide (wearing gloves if they are still hot) and the draft will fan the fire. Before you resume cooking, heap the coals together.

22 COOLING DOWN THE FIRE

If the fire is producing too much heat for your cooking needs and you want to slow it down, first close any vents that are wide open to the half-open position, wearing fireproof gloves. If the barbecue has a cover, put it on. If this doesn't work, try spreading out the coals around the grate to create a less intense bed of heat, using long-handled tongs for safety.

Tap coals against pan to remove ash

Spread out coals to disperse their heat

23 SHUTTING DOWN THE BARBECUE

When you have finished cooking, dampen down the fire to encourage it to go out of its own accord while you are eating. The hints below outline how to deal with an open-top barbecue and one with a cover and air vents.

> SPRAY THE COALS WITH WATER
If you have cooked on an open fire, spread out the coals and spray them thoroughly with water.

Stand well back from fire

< COVER THE COALS
Place the cover firmly over the cooking top to quash any flames. If the cover has a vent, close it.

> SHUT OFF THE AIR SUPPLY TO THE FUEL
Suffocate any flames by closing the air vent on the barbecue cover. Make sure that the vent on the bottom of the pan is closed, or this technique will not work.

24 REUSING OLD CHARCOAL

After cooking is finished and the barbecue has cooled down, sift through the ashes before throwing them away. Reserve any half-burned pieces of charcoal and store them in a cool, dry place for future use.

When laying out coals on the grate for your next barbecue, combine the saved old coals with a quantity of new ones; the recycled material will take longer to catch fire and will not burn as hot.

25 CLEANING THE GRILL AFTER USE

Oil the cooking surface with vegetable oil (*Tip 19, Step 1*) before use to reduce the amount of food that sticks to the grill rack. Clean the grill as soon as the barbecue is cool enough to touch, rather than

leaving it dirty and allowing food particles to set on it overnight. Use paper towels to lift surface grease, and scrape off burned remains with a small wire brush dipped in a hot solution of dish detergent.

REMOVE GREASE WITH PAPER TOWELS
Meat, poultry, and fish can leave behind a greasy residue on the grill rack. Remove this with paper towels so as not to taint the flavor of other foods you may cook.

SCRUB OFF BURNED FOODS
When foods are basted with glazes or marinades, they can leave behind charred remains. Scrub the grill surface vigorously with a wire brush to remove all traces.

MARINADES & RUBS

26 WHY MARINATE?

Meat, fish, poultry, and vegetables that have been marinated for a few hours before barbecuing will have a wonderful flavor. Also, soaking the food in liquid before cooking will make it less likely to dry out when placed over an open fire. Acidic marinades contain wine, vinegar, mustard, or citrus juice to tenderize the food; oil and paste marinades can be spread over the surface of fish or meat to form a savory protective crust that seals in juices when cooking on an open fire.

MARINADE INGREDIENTS

27 MEAT, POULTRY, GAME

Whole and cut pieces of meat, poultry, or game need longer marinating times than fish or vegetables. Place the food in a large glass bowl and pour in the marinade. Toss the meat in the mixture to coat well, and allow to absorb the flavors for up to two hours at room temperature or 48 hours in the refrigerator. Bring the food slowly back to room temperature before cooking.

▷ **MARINATING PORK SPARERIBS**
Brush off any excess marinade before cooking or it will char, and grill the ribs until they are brown with a light crust.

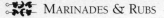
28 FRESH FISH & SHELLFISH

Whole and cut fish and shellfish are best marinated before barbecuing to prevent the flesh from drying out when subjected to the heat of the fire. Depending on the marinade you choose, fish can take on a variety of spicy and exotic flavors. Fish absorbs flavor quickly and need be marinated for only 30 minutes at room temperature, or up to two hours in the refrigerator.

▷ **MARINATING FRESH SHRIMP**
Make sure each shrimp is covered by the liquid and, when they have finished marinating, drain off the juices before placing the shrimp on the grill.

29 FRESH VEGETABLES

Like fish, most vegetables are improved with a light marinade. They need be steeped in liquid only for about 10–30 minutes at room temperature, or up to 2 hours in the refrigerator, depending on how subtle or strong a flavor you want. However, cakes of tofu – a much denser form of vegetable protein – need time for the marinade to penetrate, and are best left overnight to soak in the refrigerator.

◁ **VEGETABLES IN MARINADE**
Heap the vegetables you have ready for barbecuing in a large glass bowl, and pour in the liquid. Toss them to make sure that they are well coated.

30 VEGETABLE & HERB BRUSHES

If you do not have a long-handled brush but want to coat food cooking on the barbecue with extra marinade, try making an improvised brush out of a stick of celery or a leek, or tie together a few sprigs of rosemary and thyme into a mixed herb brush. As well as making useful tools, they will also add flavor to the food as it cooks.

Slice leek into narrow strips

Spread out sprigs to make an effective brush

△ MAKING A LEEK BRUSH
Use a sharp knife to slice up one end of the leek into a series of 2in (5cm) long strands. Spread them out to make a brush.

△ SECURING A HERB BRUSH
Trim five sprigs of herbs into 2in (5cm) lengths and wind string around one end to make a handle. Tie the string securely.

31 BASIC WINE MARINADE

For 2lb (1kg) meat, poultry, or fish

Ingredients
¼ cup (60ml) olive oil
¼ cup (60ml) wine
2 shallots, finely chopped or 1 onion, grated
2 garlic cloves, finely chopped (optional)
1 tbsp chopped fresh herbs salt and black pepper
USES
As a rule, use red wine with red meat and white with chicken or fish.

1 Combine all the ingredients in a glass bowl. Cover with plastic wrap if you are not using the marinade at once, and store chilled for 2–3 days.
2 Pour the marinade over the meat or fish of your choice, and toss to coat the food well. Steep for the recommended time (*Tips 27 & 28*) before cooking on the grill for the specified recipe time.

32 LEMON-HERB MARINADE
For 2lb (1kg) chicken, pork or fish, or 1½lb (750g) vegetables

Ingredients
3 garlic cloves, finely chopped
1 lemon, thinly sliced
juice of 1 lemon
3 tbsp olive oil
½ cup mixed fresh parsley, oregano, sage, and rosemary, finely chopped
1 tsp fennel seeds
coarsely ground salt and black pepper

GETTING AHEAD
Prepare the marinade in advance: it will keep for up to 2 days in the refrigerator.

1 Mix together all the marinade ingredients in a large glass dish.
2 Add the food; coat well. Allow to marinate (*Tips 27, 28, & 29*) before cooking.

33 SWEET-SPICY MUSTARD MARINADE
For 1½lb (750g) meat or fish

Ingredients
3 tbsp apricot jam or marmalade
1 tbsp Dijon mustard
2 tbsp honey
1 tbsp brown sugar
1 tbsp cider vinegar
1 tbsp sesame oil

USES
Marvelous for marinating chicken wings, shrimp, or lamb chops; or use as a glaze to brush onto the food just before cooking.

1 Mix together all the ingredients in a large glass dish.
2 Add the pieces of meat, chicken, or fish. Allow to marinate for the suggested time (*Tips 27 & 28*).
3 Cook quickly on a hot grill, since the sugar chars with long cooking.

34 SPICY MEXICAN MARINADE
For 2lb (1kg) meat or fish

Ingredients
3 garlic cloves, finely chopped
1 tbsp chili powder, lightly toasted
and mixed to a paste with water
1 tbsp paprika
1 tsp ground cumin
½ tsp dried oregano
2 tbsp beer or tequila
juice of 1 orange and 1 lime,
or 3 tbsp pineapple juice
2 tbsp olive oil
2 tbsp chopped fresh cilantro
coarsely ground salt, to taste
GETTING AHEAD
Prepare in advance; it will keep for
2–3 days in the refrigerator.

Ingredients
4 tbsp cooked annatto seeds, plus
2 tbsp of the cooking water
2 garlic cloves, finely chopped
½ tsp coarse salt
Spicy Mexican marinade (see above)
½ tsp ground cinnamon
½ tsp ground cloves
USES
Delicious as a marinade for
swordfish steaks or snapper.

1 Combine the ingredients in a glass dish to form a spicy red paste.
2 Add the food, turn to coat, and allow to marinate for the suggested time (*Tip 28*) before cooking.

VARIATION: ANNATTO & CHILI MARINADE
1 Purée the cooked annatto seeds and their cooking water with the garlic and salt, then mix with the spicy Mexican marinade, adding the ground cinnamon and cloves.
2 Rub the annatto mixture on both sides of the meat or fish.
3 Place in a glass dish and allow to marinate slowly at room temperature for 30–60 minutes, or in the refrigerator for up to 3 hours, before cooking on the grill.

35 TERIYAKI MARINADE

For 2lb (1kg) meat, poultry, or fish

Ingredients
¼ cup (60ml) soy sauce
¼ cup (60ml) sesame oil
¼ cup (60ml) rice wine or dry sherry
2 tbsp sugar
2 scallions, thinly sliced
2 garlic cloves, chopped
1 tsp grated ginger root

GETTING AHEAD
Prepare this Japanese-style marinade
in advance: it will keep for
2–3 days in the refrigerator.

1 Combine all the ingredients in
a glass dish, and add the food.
2 Turn the food to coat well and
allow to marinate
for the correct
time (*Tips
27 & 28*)
before
cooking.

36 HOISIN MARINADE

For 1½lb (750g) pork chops, duck breasts, or chicken thighs

Ingredients
1 cup (250ml) hoisin sauce
2–3 tbsp rice vinegar
2 tbsp soy sauce
5 garlic cloves, finely chopped
pinch of five-spice powder
1 tbsp sugar
2 tbsp sesame oil
dash of Tabasco

GETTING AHEAD
Prepare the marinade 2 days
• before your barbecue. Cover
with plastic wrap and refrigerate.

1 Combine the ingredients in a
glass bowl and add the food.
2 Turn the food to coat well and
allow to absorb the flavors for the
recommended time (*Tip 27*).
3 Remove the food, and use this
Chinese sauce as a
cooking glaze
(*Tip 42*).

37 INDONESIAN MARINADE
For 3½lb (1.75kg) chicken pieces

Ingredients
5–7 garlic cloves, finely chopped
4 scallions or 5 shallots, chopped
4 tbsp brown sugar
grated zest and juice of 2 lemons
2–3 green jalapeño chilies, finely chopped
⅓ cup (90ml) soy sauce
½ tsp turmeric
1 tbsp ground coriander
3 tbsp finely chopped ginger root
1 cup (100g) peanuts, ground or finely chopped

GETTING AHEAD
Prepare the marinade 2 days in advance of your barbecue. Cover it and store in the refrigerator.

1 Mix the ingredients in a glass dish and add the chicken pieces.
2 Turn the food to coat well and leave for 3–4 hours at room temperature, or up to 48 hours in the refrigerator for a fuller flavor.

38 TIKKA MASALA MARINADE
For 2lb (1kg) chicken pieces or 10oz (300g) firm tofu

Ingredients
2 garlic cloves, finely chopped
1 tsp chopped ginger root
2 tbsp plain yogurt
pinch of cayenne pepper
2–3 tsp cumin seeds
pinch of turmeric
1 tbsp tandoori or tikka paste
2 tbsp chopped fresh cilantro

USES
This really livens up bland foods such as tofu. The marinade will keep for up to 2 days if stored in the refrigerator.

1 Mix the ingredients together well in a large glass dish.
2 Add the chicken or tofu and turn to coat well. Allow to marinate for the suggested time
(*Tips 27 & 29*).

39 USING A DRY RUB

If you do not have time to marinate food overnight, apply a dry mixture of herbs and spices to meat, poultry, or fish about 30 minutes before cooking. Although dry rubs contain no oil to moisten or tenderize the food, the flavor will permeate the flesh. Cuts of meat are easily coated in dry rub, but other foods need help: add a splash of wine or vegetable oil to emulsify the rub and help it stick.

RUBBING SPICES INTO MEAT
Spread a layer of the mixture on a plate and lay the cut of meat on top. Press down on the meat with your fingertips to help the mix to stick. Turn the meat and repeat.

EMULSIFYING THE RUB
To help the herb and spice mixture adhere to drier foods, mix a tablespoon of wine or oil with the spices and herbs to form a smooth paste. Brush onto the food.

40 CAJUN SPICE RUB

For 2lb (1kg) meat, fish, or poultry

Ingredients
2 tbsp paprika
1 tbsp ground cumin
1 tbsp dried thyme
1 tbsp onion powder
1 tbsp garlic powder
1 tbsp dried oregano
1 tsp black pepper
1 tsp cayenne pepper

1 Place all the ingredients in a bowl and mix.
2 Sprinkle a layer of the mixture on a clean, flat surface.
3 Coat the meat, fish, or poultry on both sides. Leave for 30 minutes to absorb the flavor before barbecuing.

41 WHAT ARE PASTES & GLAZES?

Pastes and glazes are brushed over meat, fish, poultry, or vegetables before, during, and toward the end of cooking to flavor the food. They form a surface coating of flavor rather than being fully absorbed. Pastes are usually made from hot and spicy ingredients, mixed with oil or wine, while glazes use chutneys and jams combined with mustard and sugar to make a sweet caramelized topping. This works particularly well with chicken pieces and other small cuts of meat.

LEEK BRUSH

LONG-HANDLED BASTING BRUSH

42 COOKING GLAZED FOODS

Glazing barbecued foods is one of the easiest ways to liven up a simple piece of meat or poultry. Glazes can be thrown together at a moment's notice from a mixture of cupboard ingredients including mustard, sugar, and chutney. The secret of success is patience; glaze the food only when it is nearly cooked, or the sugar will burn.

1 For chicken pieces, first sear on both sides over hot coals, then cook over medium-hot coals for about 20 minutes until the skin is a crisp, golden brown and ready to be glazed before eating.

2 Taking care not to burn yourself on the hot coals, brush a thick layer of glaze over the chicken pieces. Allow it to grill for 2–3 minutes, until it starts to go sticky and becomes slightly charred.

43 MANGO-MUSTARD GLAZE
For a 4lb (2kg) duck, or 1½lb (750g) chops or kebabs

Ingredients
2½ tbsp mango chutney
1½ tbsp Dijon mustard
1½ tbsp marmalade or apricot jam
several drops of Tabasco
or other hot sauce

GETTING AHEAD
Prepare the glaze in advance:
it will keep for up to 2 weeks
in the refrigerator.

1 Mix all the ingredients together
in a glass bowl and reserve.
2 When the food is almost cooked,
brush on the glaze and continue
cooking until the glaze is sticky
and just charred.

44 MEXICAN CHILI PASTE
For 3½lb (1.75kg) chicken

Ingredients
grated zest and juice of 1 orange,
1 lime, and 1 lemon
5 garlic cloves, finely crushed
3 tbsp mild chili powder
1 tbsp paprika
1 tsp ground cumin
½ tsp dried oregano
¼ tsp ground cinnamon
1 tbsp olive oil
1 tsp salt
½ green chili, chopped, or more to taste

GETTING AHEAD
Prepare the paste in advance: it will
keep for 2–3 days in the refrigerator.

1 Mix ½ teaspoon of each fruit zest
and all the juices with the other
ingredients, adding more spices if
you want an even hotter flavor.
2 Before using, allow the paste to
thicken at room
temperature for
30 minutes.

CHARGRILLED VEGETABLES

45 PARBOILING VEGETABLES

Most vegetables will cook easily on the barbecue when raw, but some tougher vegetables such as artichokes, potatoes, and whole garlic bulbs need parboiling first to soften them. Plunge them into boiling water for 8–10 minutes (5–8 minutes for garlic), then drain.

46 FIRE-BAKED POTATOES

Serves 4 as an appetizer

Ingredients

4 medium-large baking potatoes, washed but unpeeled vegetable oil, for brushing olives, salad leaves, and sour cream with chives and shallots, to serve

1 Light the coals well before cooking, or preheat a gas barbecue.
2 Prick the potatoes once or twice with a metal skewer so that they won't burst during cooking, then brush the skins with a little oil.
3 Put the potatoes on the grill over medium-cool coals and leave, preferably covered, for 40–60 minutes, turning occasionally to make sure that they cook evenly. Alternatively, place them in a mound of slow coals and leave for 1–2 hours, until they are soft inside when tested with a skewer.
4 Cut into wedges and serve hot with olives, a green salad, and sour cream mixed with finely chopped chives and shallots.

47 FIRE-COOKED SHALLOTS

Serves 4 as a side dish

Ingredients

16 large shallots, unpeeled
3 tbsp olive oil
salt and black pepper

1 Light the barbecue coals well in advance so that they are medium-cool for cooking, or preheat a gas barbecue. Soak 4 wooden skewers in cold water for 30 minutes to prevent them from burning when placed on the grill.
2 Meanwhile, put the shallots in boiling water and blanch them for 2–3 minutes to remove their brown outer skins. Rinse well in cold water, drain again, and their skins should come away.
3 Thread the shallots onto the prepared skewers, allowing 4 per skewer, and brush both sides with olive oil. Cook the shallots on the grill over a medium-cool fire for about 10–15 minutes, turning occasionally but allowing them to char lightly on the outside.
4 Remove the shallots from the skewers, season with salt and pepper, and serve immediately.

48 FIRE-ROASTED CHERRY TOMATOES

Serves 4 as a side dish

Ingredients

40 cherry tomatoes
salt, 2 tbsp olive oil, and
2–3 garlic cloves, finely chopped
herb-flavored butter (Tips 86–90),
to serve (optional)

1 Light the barbecue in advance so that the coals are medium-hot for cooking or preheat a gas barbecue. Soak 8 wooden skewers in cold water for 30 minutes.
2 Carefully thread 5 of the cherry tomatoes onto each skewer.
3 Place the filled skewers on the grill and roast over medium-hot coals (covered if possible to control the heat) for about 5–8 minutes or until the tomato skins are just starting to split and the tomatoes are heated through.
4 Serve the fire-roasted tomatoes as soon as they are ready.
5 Remove them from the skewers onto a serving platter or side plates with care, since they will be very soft. Sprinkle with salt, olive oil, and chopped garlic, or dab with a few flecks of herb-flavored butter.

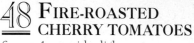

49 CLASSIC CHARGRILLED VEGETABLES
Serves 4–6 as a side dish or 2–3 as a main course

Ingredients
*2 medium-sized artichokes,
halved and chokes removed*
4 garlic bulbs
8 large tomatoes, halved
2 fennel bulbs, halved or quartered
½lb (250g) asparagus, ends trimmed
4 scallions, trimmed
2 zucchini, sliced lengthwise
*2 ears of corn, cut into
bite-sized lengths*
8 baby pattypan squash, halved
*1 each green, red, and yellow peppers,
cored, seeded, and cut into
thick strips or quarters*
*2–3 tbsp chopped mixed fresh herbs,
such as basil, parsley, oregano, rosemary,
thyme, savory, or marjoram*
Garlic Marinade
¾ cup (175ml) olive oil
¼ cup (60ml) lemon juice or wine vinegar
salt and black pepper
4–6 garlic cloves, finely chopped
*1–2 tbsp fresh chopped rosemary or
1 tsp dried herbs, such as
herbes de Provence*

1 Parboil the artichoke halves for 8–10 minutes in boiling water, drain, and place in a shallow dish.
2 Blanch the garlic bulbs in boiling water for 5–8 minutes, then drain.
3 Make the garlic marinade: place the olive oil, lemon juice, seasoning, garlic, and herbs in a bowl and mix well. Spoon about 4 tablespoons of the marinade over the parboiled artichoke halves.
4 Place the garlic and other chopped fresh vegetables in a large bowl and pour in the marinade. Toss the vegetables in the liquid and leave for 30 minutes at room temperature.
5 Light the barbecue shortly before cooking, or preheat a gas barbecue.
6 Drain the vegetables, reserving the marinade. Cook the vegetables over hot coals, turning once. As they are ready, remove them to a plate and sprinkle with reserved marinade and fresh herbs.

50 MEDITERRANEAN KEBABS

Serves 4 as a side dish or 2 as a main course

Ingredients

3–4 zucchini, cut crosswise into
½in (1cm) slices
1 large yellow pepper, cored, seeded,
and cut into bite-sized pieces
16 cherry tomatoes
2 onions, cut into chunks
several sprigs of marjoram or thyme
Mediterranean Marinade
5 garlic cloves, finely chopped
3 tbsp balsamic vinegar
⅓ cup (90ml) olive oil
2 tbsp chopped fresh marjoram or thyme
salt and black pepper, to taste

1 Light the barbecue or preheat a gas barbecue. Soak 8 wooden skewers in cold water for 30 minutes to prevent them from burning on the hot grill.
2 Thread each vegetable onto the skewers in turn, followed by an herb sprig, and place in a shallow dish.
3 Mix the marinade ingredients and pour over all the vegetable kebabs. Allow to marinate for 30 minutes at room temperature.
4 Drain the kebabs, reserving the marinade, and cook on the grill over hot coals for about 5 minutes on each side. Serve hot, removed from the skewers and with the reserved marinade poured over.

SOAKING WOODEN SKEWERS
Wooden skewers are ideal for barbecuing meat and vegetable (or even fruit) kebabs because, unlike metal skewers, they do not become too hot to handle when cooking on the grill, and so can be picked up for turning. However, wooden skewers can burn on hot fires. To prevent this, plan ahead and allow the skewers to soak in cold water for 30 minutes before cooking so that they remain damp on the grill and do not burn.

51 GRILLED ASPARAGUS

Serves 4 as an appetizer or side dish

Ingredients
1–1½lb (500–700g) asparagus tips
White Wine Marinade
½ cup (125ml) olive oil
2 tbsp lemon juice or balsamic vinegar
2 tbsp dry white wine
1 tbsp whole-grain, Dijon, or other French mustard
2 garlic cloves, finely chopped
large pinch of chopped fresh thyme or marjoram
salt and black pepper, to taste

1 Light the barbecue in advance so that it is medium-hot for cooking, or preheat a gas barbecue.
2 Mix together all the marinade ingredients in a shallow dish. Add the asparagus tips and coat well, then allow to marinate for 15–20 minutes at room temperature.
3 When the barbecue is ready, drain the asparagus tips and cook for about 3 minutes on each side, depending on the heat of the fire.

52 GRILLED EGGPLANT SLICES

Serves 4 as an appetizer or side dish

Ingredients
1 large or 2 small to medium eggplants, cut crosswise into ½in (1cm) slices
olive oil, for basting
2 tbsp red or white wine vinegar, or to taste
½ onion, finely chopped
3–4 tbsp chopped fresh parsley
salt and black pepper, to taste

1 Light the barbecue in advance so that the coals are medium-hot for cooking, or preheat a gas barbecue.
2 Brush the eggplant slices with olive oil on both sides. Cook over medium-hot coals until the first side has brown grill marks, then turn and cook the other side.
3 Remove from the heat and dress the slices with a little each of chopped onion, parsley, and seasoning. Allow the slices to cool slightly before serving at room temperature.

USING COOKED SLICES
When you have grilled the slices of eggplant, purée the smoky flesh in a food processor with a bit of freshly squeezed lemon juice to make an appetizing dip.

53 BRUSCHETTA

Serves 4 as an appetizer

Ingredients
*4 thick slices of country bread,
such as ciabatta
4 garlic cloves, halved
extra-virgin olive oil,
to taste
salt, to taste (optional)
Toppings, to serve
(see below)*

1 Light the barbecue in advance so that the coals are medium-hot for cooking, or preheat a gas barbecue.
2 Toast the bread slices on both sides over medium-hot coals until crisp and golden brown.
3 Rub both sides of each slice with the cut garlic. Drizzle with olive oil and serve with one of the following topping suggestions.

BRUSCHETTA WITH HERBS

◁ **TOMATOES & BASIL**
Top with slices of fire-roasted cherry tomatoes (Tip 48) and garnish with fresh basil.

◁ **EGGPLANT SLICES & MOZZARELLA**
Layer generous slices of mozzarella and chargrilled eggplant slices on the toast.

▷ **SWEET PEPPERS**
Chargrill yellow peppers (Tip 49) and cut them into fine slivers to make a simple, colorful, and delicious topping for bruschetta.

▷ **MOZZARELLA & BASIL**
For a quick, appetizing snack, arrange two slices of buffalo mozzarella on warm bruschetta, and sprinkle with chopped fresh basil.

△ **TAPENADE & ARUGULA**
Olive paste (tapenade) garnished with fresh arugula leaves is a perfect foil to garlicky toasted bruschetta.

BARBECUED FISH

54 FISH COOKING TIMES

Being cooked on an open fire enhances all kinds of fresh fish and shellfish. Cooking times, which vary, depend on the thickness of the flesh and whether there is a shell or not.

- **Whole fish or steaks:** Cook over hot coals for 10 minutes per 1in (2.5cm) of thickness. Cook whole fish in a basket to keep it intact.
- **Filets:** Cook for 2–3 minutes per side in a hinged basket (*Tip 55*).
- **Kebabs:** Cook over medium-hot coals for about 5 minutes per side, depending on the heat of the fire.

- **Jumbo shrimp:** Place on wooden skewers and then cook over hot coals for 5–10 minutes per side.
- **Clams & mussels:** Cook covered over hot coals. Allow 8–10 minutes for mussels, 10–12 for clams.
- **Lobster & crab:** Allow 10–15 minutes over hot coals, but do not overcook.

55 WAYS TO COOK FISH

Fish is more fragile than meat and poultry and tends to fall apart quite easily during cooking. When grilling fish on a barbecue, it is important to be able to turn the fish easily without it sticking to the grill and breaking.

Fish pieces can be secured on wooden or metal skewers (*Tip 61*), while fragile filets are best cooked in a hinged wire basket so that they can be easily turned with a minimum of fuss. Whole fish can be grilled in a specially designed fish-shaped wire basket (*Tip 56*) or wrapped in vine leaves (*Tip 57*).

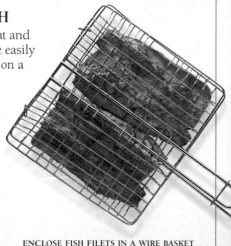

ENCLOSE FISH FILETS IN A WIRE BASKET

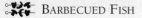
56 GRILLING LARGER FISH WHOLE

Larger fish such as snapper and sea bass are best cooked in a rigid wire basket to keep the fish whole. Cut 2 or 3 diagonal slashes on both sides of the fish so that the smoky flavor penetrates.

FISH BASKET

57 WRAPPING FISH IN GRAPE LEAVES

When fish is wrapped in grape leaves for cooking, its flesh stays moist since the fish does not come into direct contact with the fire. The leaves also add a delicious flavor.

Stuff with rolled-up grape leaves and sage

1 ▷ Clean (and, if necessary, scale) the fish. Hold it open and fill the cavity with a stuffing of your choice to enhance the flavor when cooked.

2 △ Spread out 2–3 grape leaves on a clean, dry surface and place the fish in the middle. Leaving the head and tail free, carefully wrap the leaves around the fish, covering up any exposed skin.

3 △ Secure the leaves in place with string tied around the fish at regular intervals. Fasten each piece of string with a knot. Trim the ends of the string, and take the fish to the fire for cooking.

58 CHARGRILLED SARDINES
Serves 4 as a main course

Ingredients
2lb (1kg) whole sardines or sprats, cleaned only if larger than 4–5in (10–12cm)
3 garlic cloves, finely chopped
juice of ½ lemon
2 tbsp Pernod, ouzo, or other liqueur flavored with anise
3 tbsp olive oil
2 tbsp chopped fresh parsley
salt and black pepper
lemon wedges, to garnish
raw fennel and red pepper strips, dressed with vinaigrette, to serve

1 Place the fish in a large shallow dish and add the garlic, lemon juice, Pernod, olive oil, and half the chopped parsley. Turn to coat the fish well in the liquid, then allow to marinate for 30–60 minutes at room temperature.

2 Light the coals in advance so that they are hot for cooking, or preheat a gas barbecue.

3 Drain the sardines, discarding the marinade, and cook the fish quickly over the hot coals for about 3–4 minutes on each side, until they show grill marks on the skin and the flesh is cooked through. (If the fish are grilled on a covered barbecue, they may not need turning.)

4 Season the cooked fish well, then serve hot off the grill, garnished with wedges of fresh lemon and sprinkled with the remaining parsley. Serve with a salad of raw fennel and red peppers.

59 THAI-STYLE SHRIMP

Serves 4 as an appetizer or 2 as a main course

Ingredients

12 or 24 (appetizer or main course) raw tiger shrimp in their shells, heads removed

1 walnut-sized piece of creamed coconut blended with ¼ cup (60ml) water or ¼ cup (60ml) unsweetened coconut milk

red chilies, to garnish

Thai Marinade

¼ red pepper, cored, seeded, and finely chopped

4 garlic cloves, finely chopped

2 tbsp chopped fresh cilantro

2 tbsp vinegar

juice of 2 limes

1 stalk lemon grass, finely chopped, or grated rind of ¼ lemon

½ tsp turmeric, or to taste

¼ cup (60ml) vegetable oil

pinch of ground cumin

1–2 fresh green chilies, finely chopped

½ tsp crushed dried red chilies or red chili paste

1 tsp sugar, or to taste

1 Light the barbecue in advance so that it is medium-hot, or preheat a gas barbecue.

2 Combine all the marinade ingredients in a bowl. Place the tiger shrimp in a shallow dish and pour in the marinade. Turn until well coated, then leave for 30 minutes at room temperature.

3 Soak 4 or 8 wooden skewers in cold water for 30 minutes to stop them from burning.

4 Drain the shrimp, reserving the marinade. Thread 3 shrimp on each skewer, piercing each shrimp in two places. Cook over medium-hot coals for about 2–3 minutes on each side, basting once or twice with the marinade, until the shrimp are pink and slightly charred.

5 Meanwhile, pour the reserved marinade into a small pan, stir in the coconut liquid, and heat until the sauce thickens (about 5 minutes). To serve, pour the hot sauce over the shrimp.

60 FISH FROM THE GREEK ISLANDS
Serves 6–8 as a main course

Ingredients
2 whole fish, such as
red or gray mullet, red
snapper, or tilapia, about
2lb (1kg) each
juice of 2 lemons
salt and black pepper
½ cup (125ml) olive oil
6 bay leaves, plus extra
to garnish
1 tsp dried oregano,
crumbled

1 Light the barbecue in advance so
that the coals are hot for cooking.
2 With a sharp knife, score the fish diagonally
at 2in (5cm) intervals. Rub the fish inside and
out with half the lemon juice, salt and pepper,
and 2 tablespoons of the olive oil. Place 3 bay
leaves inside each fish, and sprinkle both inside
and out with the dried oregano.
3 Secure the fish in a wire basket and cook for
about 15 minutes on each side over hot coals.
4 Sprinkle the cooked fish with the remaining
lemon juice and oil, and garnish with bay leaves.

61 MONKFISH KEBABS
Serves 4–6 as a main course

Ingredients
1½lb (750g) monkfish
steaks, cut into
about 30 chunks
salt, to taste
2 tbsp olive oil
Aïoli
1 garlic clove, crushed
1 large egg
1 tbsp Dijon mustard
juice of ½ lemon
salt and cayenne pepper,
to taste
¾–1 cup (200–250ml)
olive oil
TAKE HEED
Aïoli contains
uncooked egg.

1 Light the barbecue
in advance so that
the coals are hot
for cooking.
2 To make aïoli,
blend the garlic in a
food processor with
the whole egg, mustard,
lemon juice, salt, and
cayenne pepper.
3 Slowly add the olive oil to the
mixture, a drop at a time. Once half the oil has
been blended in, add the rest in a thin stream.
Blend until thickened, then refrigerate.
4 Thread the chunks of monkfish onto skewers.
Sprinkle with salt and brush with olive oil. Cook
over hot coals for 3–4 minutes on each side.
Serve with the aïoli and Mojo rojo (*Tip 92*).

62 GRILLED SALMON WITH LEEKS

Serves 4 as a main course

Ingredients

8 baby leeks, cleaned and trimmed
4 x 1in (2.5cm) thick salmon steaks,
about ½lb (250g) each
3 tbsp olive oil or melted butter
salt and black pepper
Chive, Lemon, & Watercress Butter
4 tbsp butter, softened
1 garlic clove, finely chopped
1 shallot, finely chopped
2 tbsp chopped chives
1 small bunch watercress, chopped
juice of ½ lemon
salt and black pepper

1 Light the barbecue in advance so that the coals are medium-hot for cooking, or preheat a gas barbecue.
2 While you are waiting, make the flavored butter. Blend the softened butter with the garlic, shallot, chives, and watercress, then stir in the lemon juice and seasoning. Drain off any excess liquid, and mold the butter into a log. Wrap in plastic wrap and chill in the refrigerator until firm.
3 Blanch the leeks in boiling water for about 2 minutes, then drain, refresh under cold running water, and drain again, to remove their outer layer.
4 Brush the salmon and the leeks with olive oil or melted butter. Season with salt and pepper.
5 Place the fish steaks and leeks directly on the grill and cook for 3–5 minutes on each side, until the salmon is firm and the leeks are just charred.
6 Serve at once with a slice of the chilled butter on top of each salmon steak.

63 SWORDFISH WITH ANNATTO & CHILI

Serves 4 as a main course

Ingredients

Annatto & chili marinade
and Spicy Mexican
marinade (Tip 34)
½ tsp crushed stick cinnamon
½ tsp ground cloves
4 swordfish steaks, about
1½lb (750g) total weight
handful of fresh bay leaves,
to scent the barbecue
bay leaves and lemon
slices, to garnish
diced onion, avocado,
tomatoes, pickled chilies,
and chopped fresh cilantro,
to serve

1 Mix together both marinades, adding the cinnamon and cloves. Rub the mixture on both sides of the fish. Leave for 30 minutes at room temperature or for up to 3 hours in the refrigerator, so that the spicy rub can permeate the flesh of the fish.

2 Light the barbecue and place the bay leaves on the coals to produce fragrant smoke (*Tip 12*).

3 Cook the fish over medium-hot coals for about 5 minutes on each side or until it is golden brown and slightly charred.

4 Mix the onion, avocado, tomatoes, chilies, and cilantro. Serve alongside the fish.

64 CAJUN FISH & GOLDEN ZUCCHINI

Serves 4 as a main course

Ingredients

4 cod filets, about
1½lb (750g) total weight
Cajun spice rub (Tip 40)
2 yellow zucchini, sliced
into ⅛in (3mm) thick strips
Sundried tomato & basil
butter (Tip 88), to serve
2 scallions,
thinly sliced, and 1–2 tbsp
chopped fresh cilantro, to
sprinkle on the cooked fish
and zucchini strips

1 Using three-quarters of the Cajun spice rub, coat the cod filets on both sides. Allow the dry rub to flavor the fish for at least 30 minutes at room temperature.

2 Light the barbecue or preheat a gas barbecue.

3 Place the cod filets in a wire basket so that they do not disintegrate on the grill, and cook over hot coals, allowing 2–3 minutes on each side or until the filets flake easily.

4 When the fish is half cooked, dust the strips of zucchini with the remaining Cajun spice rub and place on the grill. Cook for 2–3 minutes, turning several times, until lightly charred.

BARBECUED POULTRY

65 CHICKEN COOKING TIMES

Use this guide to ensure that your chicken is thoroughly cooked.
- **Pieces:** Sear on both sides over hot coals, then cook on medium-hot coals; dark meat takes 30 minutes; white meat, 15 minutes.
- **Breasts, boned:** Cook quickly over medium-hot coals for about 2–3 minutes per side.
- **Half:** Cook, covered, over medium-hot heat for 30 minutes.
- **Whole:** Cook, covered, over moderate heat (135°F/55°C) for about 1–1½ hours.

CHICKEN WINGS

- **Chicken wings:** Cook directly over hot or medium-hot coals for about 10 minutes per side.

66 HOW TO TEST IF POULTRY IS DONE

The skin of chicken, turkey, and duck soon turns a crispy golden brown when grilled on a barbecue, so it is difficult to tell whether the meat is properly cooked on the inside. Caution is needed since raw poultry carries salmonella. A good test is to pierce the flesh with a skewer. As you pull it out, check to see that the juices run clear – a sign that the flesh is thoroughly cooked.

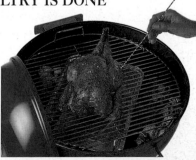

PIERCE LEG WITH A SKEWER TO TEST

67 TUSCAN CHICKEN
Serves 4 as a main course

Ingredients

*3lb (1.5kg) whole chicken,
cut into 8 pieces*
*1 yellow and 1 red pepper,
cored, seeded, and
cut into wedges*
*4 small zucchini, sliced
lengthwise*
*1lb (500g) asparagus,
ends trimmed*
black olives, to garnish
Tuscan Marinade
*10 garlic cloves,
finely chopped*
juice of 3 lemons
*2–3 tbsp chopped
fresh rosemary*
salt and black pepper
⅓ cup (90ml) olive oil
Aïoli (Tip 61), to serve

1 To make the marinade, combine the garlic, lemon juice, rosemary, a good pinch of salt, some black pepper, and the olive oil in a small bowl. Mix well to blend.
2 Place the chicken pieces in a large shallow dish. Pour two-thirds of the marinade over the chicken. Reserve the rest of the marinade to use with the accompanying vegetables. Allow the chicken to marinate for a minimum of 2 hours (or up to 48 hours) in the refrigerator.
3 Light the barbecue or preheat a gas barbecue.
4 When the coals are medium-hot, arrange the chicken on the grill. Put dark meat on the grill first since it takes longer to cook than white meat (*Tip 65*). Move the pieces around so that they cook evenly. If the barbecue has a cover, use it to create a more even temperature.
5 When the chicken is almost done (make sure by piercing the thickest part of the flesh with a skewer, *Tip 66*), toss the peppers, zucchini, and asparagus in half the reserved marinade. Arrange the vegetables on the grill and cook for about 2 minutes on each side, basting them with the rest of the marinade.
6 To serve, pile the vegetables around the chicken pieces. Garnish with black olives and serve with aïoli.

TAKE HEED
Aïoli contains uncooked egg. Do not serve it to the elderly, young children, or pregnant women.

68 CHICKEN WINGS SATAY

Serves 4 as an appetizer

Ingredients

2lb (1kg) chicken wings
6 garlic cloves,
  finely chopped
2 tbsp chopped ginger root
⅓–½ cup (90–125g) sugar,
  or to taste
¼ cup (60ml) dry sherry
  or rice wine
½ cup (125ml) dark
  soy sauce
2 tbsp sesame oil
6 scallions
Indonesian peanut sauce
(Tip 91), to serve

1 Place the chicken wings, garlic, ginger, sugar, sherry, soy sauce, and sesame oil in a shallow dish. Toss well, then cover and marinate for not less than 3 hours at room temperature.
2 Light the coals in advance, so that they are hot for cooking, or preheat a gas barbecue.
3 Grill the chicken wings for about 10 minutes a side, or until browned and crisp. A minute or two before the end of cooking, add the scallions to the grill. Serve the Indonesian peanut sauce as a dip alongside the chicken wings.

69 STUFFING A CHICKEN BREAST

A simple and quick way to enhance the flavor of chicken breasts to be cooked on the grill is to stuff them with ingredients full of flavor, such as wild mushrooms. These steps show you how.

1 Using a sharp knife, cut a deep lengthwise slit into the raw chicken breast to form a large pocket for the stuffing.

2 Open up the pocket in the flesh with the knife, and carefully spoon 3 or 4 teaspoons of the stuffing into the pocket.

3 To prevent stuffing from falling out, fasten the opening by skewering two or three times with toothpicks.

70 CHICKEN WITH MUSHROOMS
Serves 4 as a main course

Ingredients
6–8 fresh or dried morels
6–8 cepes (porcini) or
6 slices dried cepes
4 boned and skinned
chicken breasts
1 shallot, chopped
2 garlic cloves, finely chopped
2 tbsp olive oil
juice of ¼ lemon
salt and black pepper
Shallot butter (Tip 89) with 1 tbsp
seeded, chopped fresh red chili
mixed in, to serve
salad leaves and chives, to garnish

1 If using dried morels and cepes, rehydrate them by soaking them in boiling water for 30 minutes. Then drain the mushrooms and squeeze out any excess liquid. Coarsely chop the rehydrated or fresh mushrooms and set aside.

2 Light the barbecue or preheat a gas barbecue.

3 Cut a pocket lengthwise in each chicken breast, then fill each with a quarter of the chopped mushrooms (*Tip 69*). Arrange the stuffed breasts in a shallow glass dish.

4 Mix together the shallot, garlic, olive oil, lemon juice, salt, and pepper. Pour over the chicken breasts and turn to coat well. Cover and allow to marinate at room temperature for at least 1 hour.

5 Cook the stuffed chicken breasts over hot coals for at least 4 minutes a side, until they are cooked through and the juices run clear when pierced with a skewer (*Tip 66*). Avoid overcooking. Serve with slices of Shallot butter (*Tip 89*) and garnish with salad leaves and sprigs of chives.

71 CHICKEN TIKKA KEBABS

Serves 4 as a main course

Ingredients

*4 boned, skinned chicken breasts,
about 2lb (1kg) total weight,
cut into bite-sized pieces
juice of 1 lemon
2 tbsp butter, melted
Tikka Marinade
⅔ cup (150g) plain yogurt
3 garlic cloves, finely chopped
2 tsp ground coriander
½ tsp turmeric
1½ tsp ground cumin
1½ tbsp paprika
¼ tsp ground ginger
large pinch of cayenne pepper
1 tbsp tamarind paste or mango chutney*

1 Arrange the chicken pieces in a shallow dish, pour in the lemon juice, and allow to tenderize for 15–30 minutes.
2 Mix together all the marinade ingredients, pour over the chicken, and turn to coat well. Cover; leave for up to 3 hours at room temperature.
3 Light the barbecue.
4 Thread the chicken onto soaked wooden skewers, and brush with the butter.
5 Cook over hot coals, preferably covered, for about 3 minutes a side.

72 HOW TO SPLIT POULTRY

The technique described here is used to make a whole chicken or game hen an even thickness so that all parts of the bird will cook at the same rate, preventing thinner parts of the flesh from drying out.

1 Using a strong pair of kitchen scissors, remove the backbone by cutting along one side and then the other.

2 Lay the chicken skin-side down and press down firmly on the bird with the heel of your hand to flatten it out.

3 To hold the chicken flat while it cooks, secure the wings and legs in place with a crisscross of bamboo skewers.

73 GRILLED GAME HENS & HERBS

Serves 4 as a main course

Ingredients
4 tbsp unsalted butter
1½ tbsp aromatic wine vinegar,
such as rosemary or garlic
4 garlic cloves, finely chopped
4 game hens, split (Tip 72)
salt and black pepper
2 tsp mixed dried herbs, including thyme,
marjoram, rosemary, fennel, and savory
½ tsp crumbled dried bay leaves
½oz (15g) fresh basil leaves,
torn into pieces
fresh rosemary sprigs, to garnish

1 Light the barbecue coals well in advance, or preheat a gas barbecue.
2 Over a low barbecue heat, melt half the butter in a small pan. Add the vinegar and garlic and cook for 1–2 minutes, then set aside.
3 Season the game hens, rubbing in the salt and pepper, then brush the skins with the melted butter and sprinkle with dried herbs.
4 To flavor the flesh, loosen the skin in places along the breast and thighs and stuff with flecks of the unmelted butter and torn basil leaves. Then, make small cuts over the rest of the skin and insert more butter and basil as before. Cover and leave the game hens for 30–60 minutes at room temperature.
5 Barbecue the game hens over medium-hot coals for 20–30 minutes, until golden brown on the outside but still moist inside, turning occasionally. The game hens are cooked if the juices run clear when the thigh is pierced with a skewer (*Tip 66*). Serve garnished with rosemary sprigs.

BARBECUED MEAT

74 HOW LONG TO COOK?

The cooking times described here will help you judge how long to cook small cuts of meat on the barbecue. When cooking large cuts, use a meat thermometer to determine the cooking time more accurately.

MEAT
THERMOMETER

BEEF COOKING TIMES

- **Hamburgers** Cook over medium-hot coals for 3 minutes on one side. Turn and cook the hamburgers for a further 3 minutes for rare or up to 10 minutes for well done.
- **Steaks** Sear for 1 minute per side, then cook for 4 minutes per side for rare or up to 8 for well done.
- **Beef (or lamb) kebabs** Cook over medium-hot coals for 3–4 minutes per side for rare or up to 6–7 minutes if you like your meat well done.

LAMB COOKING TIMES

- **Lamb chops** For 1–1½in (2.5–3.5cm) thick chops, sear and cook over medium-hot coals for 4–5 minutes per side for rare or up to 8 for well done.

PORK COOKING TIMES

- **Loin or rib chops** For 1in (2.5cm) thick chops, sear both sides, then cook, covered, over medium-hot coals for 6–8 minutes per side.
- **Spareribs** Cook, preferably covered, over medium-hot, indirect heat until tender (1–2 hours for rack ribs), then directly over the heat to char. Alternatively, precook ribs in foil, then barbecue over hot coals for about 10 minutes per side.
- **Kebabs** Cook either covered or uncovered over medium-hot coals for 5–6 minutes per side (the meat should be cooked right through).

SAUSAGE COOKING TIMES

- **Beef, lamb, pork, or veal** Prick the skins, then cook over medium-hot coals for about 5 minutes per side. Cook pork sausages for an extra 3 minutes per side.

75 ALL-AMERICAN RIBS
Serves 4 as a main course

Ingredients
*2lb (1kg) pork spareribs,
either in a rack or separated
4 leeks, cut into brushes
(Tip 30), for basting*
Down-home Dry Rub
*1 tbsp onion powder
1 tbsp salt
1 tsp black pepper
3 tbsp paprika
1 tbsp dry mustard
1 tbsp garlic powder
1 tbsp crumbled dried
bay leaves*
Lone Star Moppin' Sauce
*⅔ cup (150ml) cider vinegar
⅓ cup (90ml) vegetable oil
¼ cup (60ml)
Worcestershire sauce
½ tsp Tabasco or other
hot sauce
1 tbsp paprika
1 tbsp mild chili powder
1 tsp mustard powder
1 tsp crumbled dried
bay leaves
1 tsp garlic powder
½ tsp celery salt, or to taste
She-devil barbecue sauce
(Tip 95), for brushing*

1 Mix the dry rub ingredients together in a bowl. Dust the ribs with the mixture, then rub it in well. Leave the ribs for 30 minutes at room temperature to absorb the flavor.
2 Light the barbecue well in advance so that the fire will be medium-cool for cooking, or preheat a gas barbecue.
3 To make the mopping sauce, place all the listed ingredients in a mixing bowl and blend together well.
4 Cook the ribs over cool coals. Using a leek brush, baste the spareribs from time to time on the grill with mopping sauce. If possible, cover the grill: the longer and slower the ribs cook, the more tender the meat will be. If the ribs are in a rack, allow about 1–2 hours cooking time, or 40 minutes if separated.
5 When the ribs are almost done, brush them with She-devil barbecue sauce. Serve at once, offering any remaining sauce separately.

76 CLASSIC HAMBURGERS
Serves 4 as a main course

Ingredients
1½lb (750g) lean ground beef
8 shallots or 1 onion, finely chopped
3–4 tbsp heavy cream
4 thin ice cubes
salt and black pepper
Shredded Lettuce Burger Sauce
½ cup (125g) prepared mayonnaise
3 tbsp Dijon mustard, or a combination of
brown and American yellow mustard
½ head iceberg lettuce or 1 head leaf
lettuce, shredded
4 shallots, finely chopped
juice of ½ lemon
4 sesame buns
sliced tomatoes, onions, and pickles,
to garnish

1 Light the barbecue in advance so that the coals will be hot, or preheat a gas barbecue.
2 Place the ground beef in a large bowl and break it up with a fork. Add the shallots and cream and beat with a wooden spoon until the mixture is well combined.
3 Using clean, wet hands so that the mixture does not stick to them, divide then flatten into patties about 1in (2.5cm) thick. Insert an ice cube into the center of each patty to keep the meat moist during cooking on the barbecue.
4 Generously season the patties with salt and pepper and place on the barbecue over hot coals. Cook for 3 minutes, then turn to cook the other side. Continue until the meat is done to taste (*Tip 74*).
5 To make the sauce, blend the mayonnaise and mustard together in a bowl. Add the lettuce and shallots, and toss until well combined. Add lemon juice to taste.
6 Split the sesame buns in half and lightly toast them on the barbecue. Serve each burger in a bun, topped with lettuce sauce. Garnish with slices of tomato, raw onion rings, and pickles.

77 SAUSAGE SELECTION

Serves 4 as a main course

Ingredients

*2lb (1kg) assorted sausages,
such as smoked kielbasa,
Toulouse, chorizo, bratwurst
4 onions, peeled and halved
1 each red, yellow, and green
peppers, halved and seeded
2 fennel bulbs, quartered
lengthwise
2–3 tbsp olive oil
juice of ½ lemon
salt and black pepper
relishes, to serve*

1 Light the barbecue or preheat a gas barbecue.
2 Prick the sausages and cook over medium-hot coals for 5 minutes per side (*Tip 74*).
3 Meanwhile, toss the vegetables in olive oil and lemon juice; season. Place around the cooler edges of the grill; cook until tender.
4 As individual sausages and vegetables are cooked through, remove from the grill and keep warm. Serve with a choice of relishes.

78 MOROCCAN LAMB BROCHETTES

Serves 4 as a main course

Ingredients

*1½lb (750g) boneless lamb
shoulder chops, cut into
bite-sized pieces
1 onion, finely chopped
5 garlic cloves, finely chopped
2 tsp crumbled dried bay
leaves or herbes de Provence
pinch of dried thyme
2 tsp ground cumin
½ tsp turmeric
juice of 1½ lemons
⅓ cup (90ml) olive oil
salt and black pepper
1 tbsp paprika
1 tbsp chopped fresh cilantro*

1 Place the lamb pieces in a dish with the onion, garlic, bay leaves, thyme, half the cumin, turmeric, lemon juice, and olive oil. Mix well, then marinate for at least 30 minutes or, if there is time, up to 3 hours at room temperature or overnight in the refrigerator.
2 Light the barbecue.
3 Thread the lamb onto soaked wooden skewers (*Tip 50*), then season to taste. Cook over hot coals until browned on one side, about 5 minutes, then turn and cook the other side for another 5 minutes.
4 Sprinkle with the remaining cumin and the paprika and cilantro, and serve.

79 CUMIN ROAST LAMB

Serves 4 as a main course

Ingredients

*4 baby leeks or small
peeled brown onions, or
8 scallions, trimmed
1lb (500g) pumpkin or
other orange winter
squash, unpeeled and cut
into ¼in (5mm) slices
1 eggplant, cut into wedges
or thick slices
2 tbsp olive oil
juice of ½ lemon
4 lamb steaks, about
6–8oz (175–250g) each
fresh cilantro leaves,
to garnish*
Cumin Paste
*2 tbsp cumin seeds
2 tbsp ground cumin
6 garlic cloves, crushed
1 tsp salt
4 tbsp olive oil
2 tbsp chopped fresh
cilantro or parsley
juice of 1 lemon*

1 Place all the cumin paste ingredients in a bowl and mix together.

2 Blanch the leeks for 1–2 minutes in boiling water, then drain. Place in a shallow dish with the pumpkin and eggplant.

3 Drizzle the vegetables with olive oil and lemon juice, then add 1–2 tablespoons of the cumin paste and toss the vegetables to coat them.

4 Place the lamb steaks in a shallow dish and add the remaining cumin paste, turning to coat well on all sides. Cover and allow the lamb and vegetables to marinate for at least 30 minutes at room temperature.

5 Light the barbecue so that the coals are hot for cooking, or preheat a gas barbecue.

6 Place the meat and vegetables on the grill over hot coals. Turn everything once or twice while cooking, so that the lamb steaks are browned on the outside but still pink inside, and the vegetables are tender and with grill marks.

7 Garnish with fresh cilantro leaves.

TO SERVE
*Accompany this dish
with Middle Eastern
spiced pilaf (Tip 101) and
Cucumber-yogurt raita
(Tip 94), if desired.*

80 FAJITAS

Serves 4 as a main course

Ingredients

½lb (250g) skirt steak or
other tender beef steak,
in one piece
Mexican chili paste
(Tip 44)
4 tbsp tequila
1 chicken breast, boned
but not skinned
2 chorizo sausages,
poached (optional)
4 small onions, unpeeled,
halved lengthwise
2 ripe plantains, peeled,
halved lengthwise
12 flour tortillas
2 tbsp sour cream
1 red chili, finely chopped
sliced limes, cilantro, and
shredded lettuce, to garnish

1 Spread about half of the Mexican chili paste over the beef, and allow to stand at room temperature for 10 minutes to absorb some of the flavor. Sprinkle over 2 tablespoons of tequila, cover the meat with plastic wrap, and place in the refrigerator to marinate overnight.

2 Spread the rest of the chili paste over the chicken breast, sprinkle with the remaining tequila, and refrigerate for at least 1–2 hours.

3 Light the barbecue.

4 Cook the beef over hot coals for 8–10 minutes, turning once, until it is cooked on the outside but still rare inside, or to taste (Tip 74).

5 When the beef is half cooked, place the whole chicken breast on the grill and cook for about 4 minutes on each side, or until the juices run clear when pierced with a skewer (Tip 66). Add the poached sausages, if using, onions, and plantains, and grill for 2–3 minutes on each side.

6 Sprinkle each tortilla with a little cold water to keep it moist, then grill for 30 seconds on each side. Keep warm in a clean dish towel.

7 Remove the onions and plantains from the grill and place them on a serving platter. Slice the beef and chicken into thin strips (cut up the sausages). Arrange all the meat (and sausages) on the platter; sprinkle with the chopped chili.

8 Serve the meat (and sausages) wrapped up in the tortillas, together with accompaniments such as sour cream, Guacamole (Tip 97), Salsa (Tip 98), and Refried beans (Tip 99). Garnish each serving with sliced limes, cilantro leaves, and shredded lettuce.

81 BEEF SHISH KEBAB

Serves 4 as a main course

Ingredients

*1½lb (750g) sirloin or other
prime cut of beef, cut into
bite-sized cubes
3–5 garlic cloves,
finely chopped
1 small onion, chopped
10 black peppercorns,
coarsely ground
1 cup (250ml) red wine
handful of fresh bay leaves
3 small onions, peeled and
cut into wedges
3 green peppers, halved,
seeded, and
cut into wedges
½ cup (125ml) sunflower oil
salt and black pepper*

1 Place the cubed beef in a glass dish with the garlic, onion, peppercorns, red wine, and bay leaves. Turn to coat, then cover and marinate for 3 hours at room temperature or overnight in the refrigerator.
2 Light the barbecue or preheat a gas barbecue.
3 Thread the meat and the bay leaves onto skewers, alternating with onion and green pepper wedges.
4 Cook over hot coals, turning occasionally. Allow about 5–7 minutes for rare, 9–10 minutes for medium-rare, and 12–13 for well done. Serve at once.

82 TUSCAN-STYLE STEAK

Serves 4 as a main course

Ingredients

*4 tender steaks,
such as filet or sirloin,
8oz (250g) each
3–4 tbsp olive oil
pinch of dried sage
or oregano
salt and black pepper
juice of 2 lemons*

1 Place the steaks in a shallow dish and pour in half the olive oil. Turn to coat, then sprinkle with the dried sage or oregano. Cover the steaks and allow to marinate at room temperature for up to 3 hours.
2 Light the barbecue or preheat a gas barbecue.
3 Grill the steaks over hot coals for about 8–10 minutes, or to taste (*Tip 74*), turning once.
4 Remove the steaks from the grill, season, then drizzle with the remaining olive oil and lemon juice to taste. Serve immediately.

83 THAI-INSPIRED PORK
Serves 4 as a main course

Ingredients

*1½lb (750g) lean pork,
such as tenderloin, cut into
thin medallions
½ cup (125ml) sherry,
port, or rice wine
½ cup (125ml)
chicken stock
2 tbsp brown sugar
2–3 tbsp lime juice*
Thai Spice Paste
*2 tbsp grated ginger root
2 tbsp medium sherry,
port, or rice wine
½ cup (60g) roasted
peanuts, coarsely chopped
or crushed
4 scallions,
thinly sliced
1 tbsp vegetable oil
1 tbsp sesame oil
1 green or red chili,
finely chopped
1½ tsp turmeric
1 tbsp brown sugar
1 tbsp balsamic or
raspberry vinegar
2 tsp ground cumin
1 medium bunch fresh
cilantro, chopped
salt, to taste
black pepper*

1 Blend the Thai spice paste ingredients together (if the nuts are salty, you may not need any extra salt, depending on taste).

2 Rub about half the spicy paste over the pork medallions, and leave for 1–3 hours at room temperature or overnight in the refrigerator.

3 Remove the meat from the paste with a slotted spoon, then place any mixture left behind in a saucepan with the sherry, chicken stock, sugar, and half the lime juice. Bring to a boil, then reduce the heat and cook to form an almost syrupy glaze.

4 Light the barbecue or preheat a gas barbecue.

5 Cook the pork over hot coals until charred on each side but juicy inside. (Medallions are thin, so this will take only 2–3 minutes on each side.)

6 To serve, add the second half of the spice paste to the glaze (*Step 3*), together with the last 1½ tbsp of lime juice. Warm this sauce through, and put a spoonful or two on each plate with the pork.

LEAFY RICE SIDE DISH
Finely slice some red chilies and scallions (green part only) and mix with freshly cooked long-grain white rice. Fold four fresh banana leaves into cones, securing with wooden cocktail sticks. Fill the cones with the rice mixture and serve as a side dish.

BUTTERS, SAUCES, & SIDE DISHES

84 FLAVORING BUTTER

Butter, flavored with a variety of herbs and spices, makes a tasty accompaniment to barbecued foods. Simply serve a slice or two of butter on top of meat, fish, or vegetables straight from the barbecue, and allow it to melt before eating. Alternatively, place a slice of flavored butter inside a hamburger before cooking, and it will baste the meat as it barbecues.

▽ **BARBECUED SALMON STEAKS**
A nugget of chive, lemon, and watercress butter on top of each grilled salmon steak (Tip 62) enhances its flavor.

Unwrap and slice the chilled roll of butter

85 HOW LONG WILL BUTTERS KEEP?

Flavored butters can be made well in advance of a barbecue. Unlike marinades and pastes, which tend to keep for only 2–3 days at most in the refrigerator, butters will keep for up to 1 week when chilled. Flavored butters can also be frozen successfully and will keep for up to 2 months in the freezer. Before freezing, first seal the freshly made butter in plastic wrap or wrap it up tightly in waxed paper. Allow the butter to defrost slowly at a cool room temperature for at least 2 hours before use.

86 ROSEMARY-MUSTARD BUTTER
For 2lb (1kg) lamb, chicken, or sliced potatoes

Ingredients

½ cup (125g) unsalted butter, softened
1 tbsp Dijon mustard
2 garlic cloves, finely chopped
2 tbsp chopped fresh rosemary
salt and black pepper

With a fork, combine the softened butter with the Dijon mustard, garlic, and rosemary, and season to taste.

87 BLACK OLIVE & SAGE BUTTER
For 2lb (1kg) turkey or hamburgers

Ingredients

½ cup (125g) unsalted butter, softened
8–10 fresh sage leaves, chopped
2–3 tbsp black olives in oil, drained,
pitted (if necessary),
and coarsely chopped
2 garlic cloves, finely chopped
salt and black pepper

With a fork, combine the softened butter with the sage, black olives, garlic, and seasoning. Serve right away or chill.

88 SUNDRIED TOMATO & BASIL BUTTER
For 2lb (1kg) chicken breast, swordfish, or salmon

Ingredients

½ cup (125g) unsalted butter, softened
4 garlic cloves, finely chopped
5–8 sundried tomatoes packed in oil,
drained, patted dry to remove
excess oil, and finely diced,
plus ½ tsp of the oil
3 tbsp finely chopped fresh basil leaves
salt and black pepper

Blend the butter, garlic, and sundried tomatoes. Work in the oil and chopped basil, then blend in some salt and pepper to taste.

89 SHALLOT BUTTER

For 1lb (500g) filet steak, shrimp, or scallops

Ingredients
½ cup (125g) unsalted butter, softened
dash of lemon juice
2 shallots, finely chopped
salt and black pepper

With a fork, combine the softened butter and lemon juice, and season with salt and pepper to taste. Serve at room temperature or chill and cut up into slices.

90 CILANTRO & CHILI BUTTER

For 1½lb (750g) shrimp

Ingredients
½ cup (125g) unsalted butter, softened
¼ cup (15g) chopped fresh cilantro
3 scallions, thinly sliced
2 garlic cloves, finely chopped
¼ green chili, or to taste,
finely chopped
dash of lime juice
pinch of grated lime zest
salt, to taste

Blend together the softened butter with the cilantro, scallions, garlic, chili, lime juice, and lime zest. Season to taste with salt. Use at once, or wrap and refrigerate or freeze (*Tip 85*).

91 INDONESIAN PEANUT SAUCE

Serve with Chicken wings (*Tip 68*)

Ingredients
4 garlic cloves, finely chopped
2 tsp chopped ginger root
½ cup (150g) crunchy peanut butter
2 tbsp sugar
4 tbsp water
Tabasco or other hot
sauce, to taste
1 tbsp lemon juice
2 tbsp soy sauce
3 tbsp chopped fresh cilantro
1 tbsp sesame oil
salt and black pepper

1 Mix the garlic with the ginger, peanut butter, and sugar.
2 Slowly stir in the water, then when emulsified add the Tabasco, lemon juice, soy sauce, cilantro, and sesame oil. Season to taste.

92 MOJO ROJO

Serve with Monkfish kebabs (*Tip 61*)

Ingredients
*1 medium-hot dried red chili,
such as cayenne or Arbol
1 tsp cumin seeds
½ cup (125ml) water
5–6 garlic cloves, finely chopped
2 tbsp paprika
½ cup (125ml) olive oil
2 tbsp red wine vinegar
salt, to taste*

1 Bring the chili, cumin seeds, and water to a boil and cook over a high heat for about 5 minutes.
2 Purée the garlic, add the chili mixture and paprika, then slowly blend in the olive oil. Add the red wine vinegar and salt, and serve.

93 RED CHILI AÏOLI

For 2lb (1kg) chicken, shrimp, eggplant, or zucchini

Ingredients
*½ cup (100g) prepared good-quality
mayonnaise
1 garlic clove, finely chopped
1 tbsp mild red chili powder
or pure mild chili powder
1 tbsp paprika
¼ tsp ground cumin
1 tbsp chopped fresh cilantro
dash of lemon or lime juice
2–3 tbsp olive oil
salt and black pepper*

1 Combine the mayonnaise with the garlic, chili powder, paprika, cumin, cilantro, and a dash of lemon or lime juice.
2 With a whisk or fork, slowly blend in the olive oil, a little at a time, until it is absorbed. Season to taste. Chill the aïoli until ready to serve.

94 CUCUMBER-YOGURT RAITA
Serve with Chicken tikka kebabs (*Tip 71*)

Ingredients
1 cup (250g) plain yogurt
½ cucumber, finely diced
2–3 garlic cloves, finely chopped
2 tbsp chopped fresh cilantro or parsley
2 tsp chopped fresh mint, plus a few sprigs to garnish
salt, to taste
pinch of cayenne pepper (optional)

Using a fork, blend all the ingredients together in a bowl and keep chilled until ready to serve. Sprinkle with cayenne pepper and garnish with fresh mint sprigs.

95 SHE-DEVIL BARBECUE SAUCE
Serve with All-American ribs (*Tip 75*)

Ingredients
1 onion, coarsely grated
3–5 garlic cloves, finely chopped
4 tbsp Worcestershire sauce
1 cup (250g) tomato ketchup
¼ cup dark brown sugar
2–3 chipotle chilies
1 cup (250ml) beer, plus extra if needed
1 cup (250ml) water, plus extra if needed
1 tsp dry mustard
1 tsp mild red chili powder
1 tsp ground cumin
salt and black pepper
¼ cup (60ml) cider vinegar

1 Combine the onion, garlic, Worcestershire sauce, ketchup, brown sugar, chipotle chilies, beer, water, mustard, chili powder, cumin, salt and pepper, and half the vinegar in a large non-reactive saucepan.
2 Bring to a boil, then reduce the heat and simmer for 30–45 minutes, or until it forms a thick, sticky sauce. If the mixture starts to burn on the pan base, add more water or beer.
3 Add the remaining cider vinegar to the sauce, and taste for seasoning. Remove from the heat.
4 When the ribs are nearly finished cooking on the grill, brush them with the barbecue sauce. Put the rest of the sauce in a bowl to dip into while eating.

96 THAI DIPPING SAUCE

Serve with meat, poultry, fish, or vegetables

Ingredients

1 cup (200g) chopped canned tomatoes, with their juice
2 tbsp dark brown sugar, or to taste
1 cup (125g) golden raisins, coarsely chopped
4 garlic cloves, finely chopped
½–1 dried red chili, crumbled
½ tsp cayenne pepper, or to taste
3 tbsp cider (or raspberry) vinegar, or to taste
salt, to taste
3 tbsp water, plus extra if needed

1 Combine the tomatoes with the brown sugar, raisins, garlic, chili, cayenne pepper, vinegar, and salt. Blend until the mixture is slightly chunky, adding water as necessary until the sauce has a slightly liquid consistency.
2 Pour the sauce into a pan and bring to a boil for a few minutes to allow the flavors to mingle.
3 When cool, add more vinegar, cayenne, salt, and sugar, to taste.

97 GUACAMOLE

Serve with Fajitas (*Tip 80*)

Ingredients

2 ripe avocados
½ onion, finely chopped
2 garlic cloves, finely chopped
2–3 tomatoes, diced
½ fresh green chili, such as jalapeño or serrano, finely chopped
juice of 1–2 limes
¼ tsp ground cumin
salt and cayenne pepper, to taste

1 Cut the avocados in half and remove the pits. Scoop out the flesh and mash coarsely.
2 Combine the avocado with all the remaining ingredients. Serve immediately, or cover tightly with plastic wrap to prevent air from turning the avocados black. Chill, and mix again well before serving.

98 SALSA

Serve with Fajitas (*Tip 80*)

Ingredients

3–5 garlic cloves, finely chopped
1 small onion, chopped
1 tbsp chopped fresh parsley
1 tbsp chopped fresh cilantro
10 ripe tomatoes, skinned and chopped
1 tsp ground cumin
1–2 jalapeño or serrano chilies, finely chopped
1 tbsp lemon juice or vinegar
salt, to taste

Combine the ingredients with a fork. Purée if you prefer a smooth salsa.

99 REFRIED BEANS

Serve with Fajitas (*Tip 80*)

Ingredients

2 cups (400g) cooked pinto beans, plus about ½ cup (125ml) of the cooking liquid
¼ cup (60ml) vegetable oil
1 onion, finely chopped
salt, to taste
¼ tsp ground cumin
large pinch of mild chili powder
½ cup (250g) grated cheese, such as mild Cheddar or Pecorino

1 Using a potato masher, carefully mash the cooked pinto beans into the cooking liquid, leaving about a third of the beans whole or partially whole, to make a chunky-textured purée.

2 Heat the oil in a large pan, add the chopped onion, and sauté until soft and translucent. Add salt to taste, sprinkle with the ground cumin and chili powder, then add about ½ cup (125ml) of the bean mixture.

3 Cook over a high heat until the bean mixture thickens and reduces in volume, then add more puréed beans, stirring and mashing as you cook.

4 When all the beans have been added to the pan and the mixture is a thick creamy purée, it is ready to serve.

5 Sprinkle the bean purée with the grated cheese and continue heating gently until the cheese melts. (You can do this on the barbecue if you want the beans to have a smoky flavor.)

100 BLACK BEAN SALSA
Serve with Swordfish (*Tip 63*)

Ingredients
6oz (175g) canned black beans, drained
2–3 ripe tomatoes, diced
1 garlic clove, finely chopped
1 scallion, finely chopped
1 red or green Thai or serrano chili, finely chopped
1 tbsp lime juice
¼ tsp ground cumin, or to taste
1–2 tbsp chopped fresh cilantro leaves
salt, to taste

Mix all the ingredients together in a bowl, season with salt to taste, and serve.

101 MIDDLE EASTERN SPICED PILAF
Serve with Cumin roast lamb (*Tip 79*)

Ingredients
¾ cup (90g) almonds, whole or slivered
4 tbsp butter
2oz (60g) thin spaghetti, broken up
2 onions, thinly sliced lengthwise
½ tsp ground cinnamon
¼ tsp ground cumin
1 cup (250g) long-grain white rice
2 cups (500ml) hot chicken stock (homemade or low-sodium)
¾ cup (100g) raisins

1 Sauté the almonds in 1 tablespoon of butter until golden brown. Remove and reserve.
2 Add another tablespoon of butter to the pan and brown the spaghetti. Remove and reserve.
3 Sauté the onions in another tablespoon of butter until soft and golden. Sprinkle with half the cinnamon and cumin. Remove and reserve.
4 Sauté the rice in the remaining butter for about 3–4 minutes. Add the stock, raisins, and remaining cinnamon and cumin. Cover and cook over low heat until the rice is half done.
5 Add the spaghetti to the pan, cover, and cook until both the rice and spaghetti are al dente, about 10 minutes. Fork in the onions and top with the almonds.

INDEX

ACKNOWLEDGMENTS

Dorling Kindersley would like to thank Hilary Bird for
compiling the index, Richard Hammond for proofreading,
Robert Campbell and Mark Bracey for DTP assistance,
Emma Patmore for preparing food for special photography, and
The Barbecue Shop, Cobham, Surrey and Landmann Ltd. for props.

Photography
Special food photography by Clive Streeter, assisted by Amy Hearn.
Special barbecue photography by Matthew Ward.
All other photographs by Dave King, Diana Miller,
David Murray, and Roger Phillips.